COMPOSER SHOWCASE
HAL LEONARD STUDENT PIANO LIBRARY

ELEMENTARY LEVEL

Just Pink

NINE PIECES FOR PIANO SOLO

BY JENNIFER LINN

T0081839

CONTENTS

ISBN 978-1-4234-3537-2

HAL•LEONARD®
CORPORATION
7777 W. BLUEMOUND RD. P.O. BOX 13819 MILWAUKEE, WI 53213

In Australia Contact:
Hal Leonard Australia Pty. Ltd.
4 Lentara Court
Cheltenham, Victoria, 3192 Australia
Email: ausadmin@halleonard.com.au

Visit Hal Leonard Online at
www.halleonard.com

Bubblegum Song

Words and Music by
Jennifer Linn

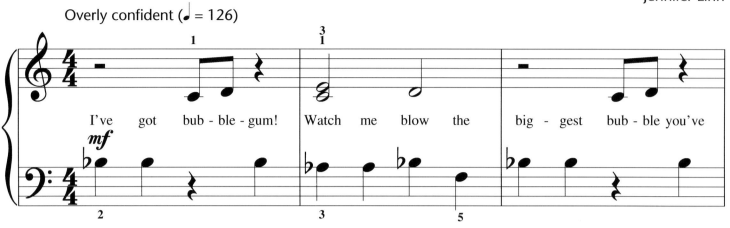

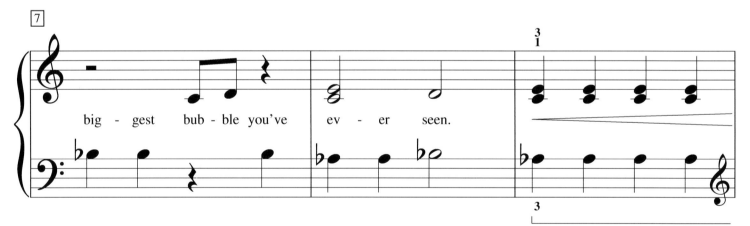

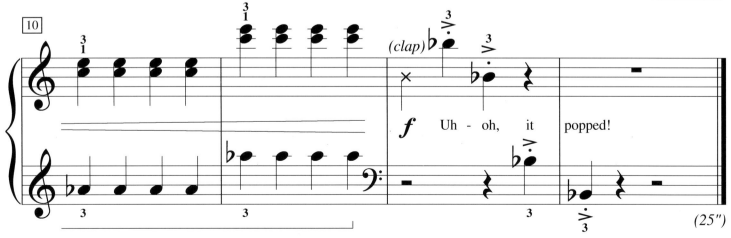

Flamingo

By Jennifer Linn

Elegant and flowing ($\quad$ = 126)

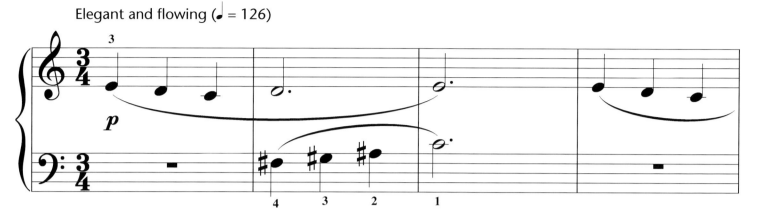

(Hold damper pedal to the end)

Both hands 8va

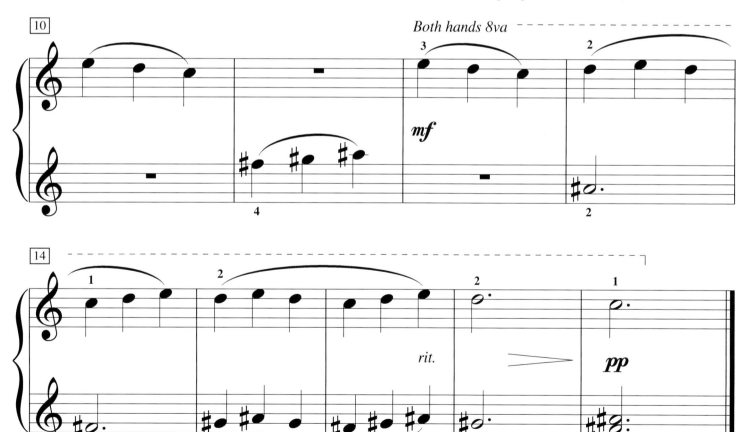

(27")

Piglet

Words and Music by
Jennifer Linn

Moderately cute (♩ = 132)

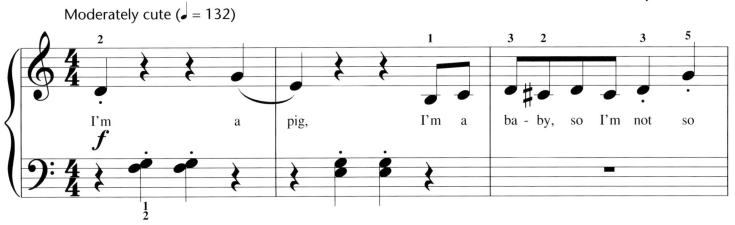

I'm   a   pig,   I'm a   ba - by, so I'm not so

big!   Pig - let is my name, and I   have a curl - y tail.

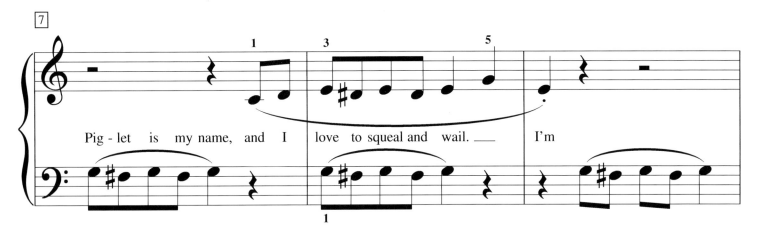

Pig - let is my name, and I   love to squeal and wail. ___   I'm

a   pig!

(22")

Pink Fuzzy Slippers

Words and Music by
Jennifer Linn

Cheerfully (♩ = 100)

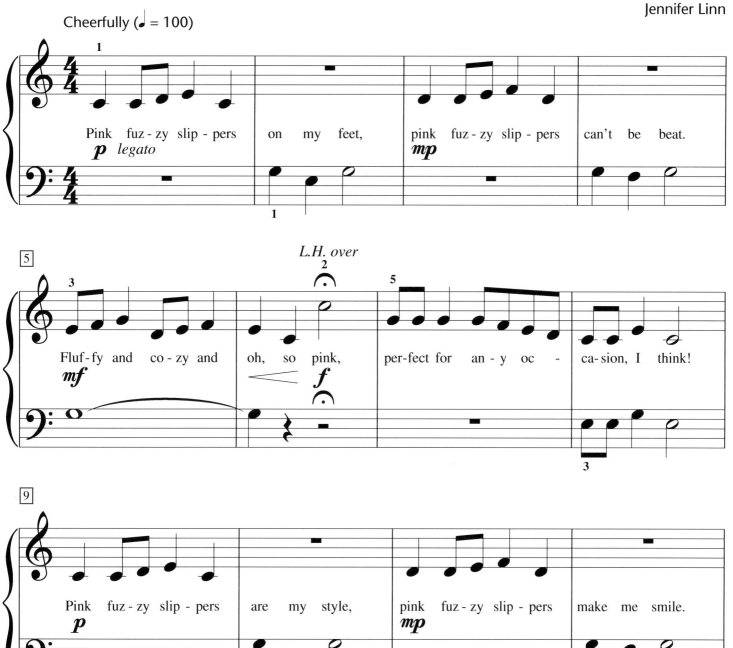

Pink fuz-zy slip-pers on my feet, pink fuz-zy slip-pers can't be beat.

Fluf-fy and co-zy and oh, so pink, per-fect for an-y oc - ca-sion, I think!

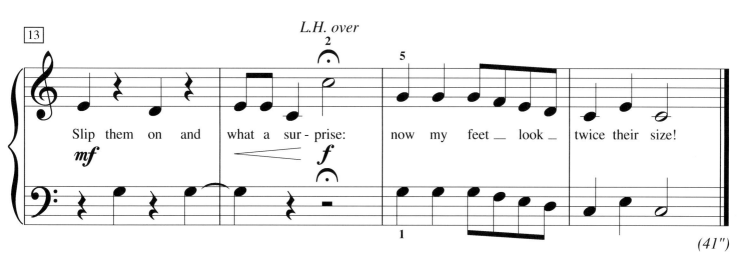

Pink fuz-zy slip-pers are my style, pink fuz-zy slip-pers make me smile.

Slip them on and what a sur-prise: now my feet __ look __ twice their size!

(41")

Pink Party Surprise

Words and Music by
Jennifer Linn

Very politely (♩ = 112)

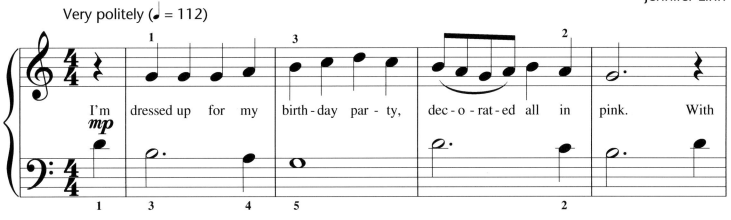

I'm dressed up for my birth-day par-ty, dec-o-rat-ed all in pink. With

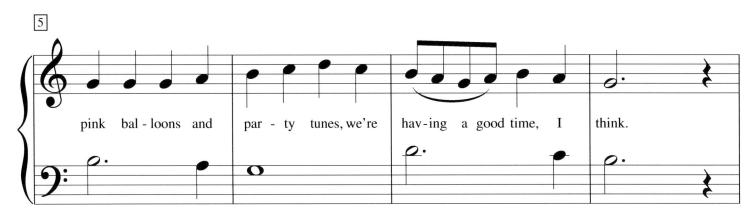

pink bal-loons and par-ty tunes, we're hav-ing a good time, I think.

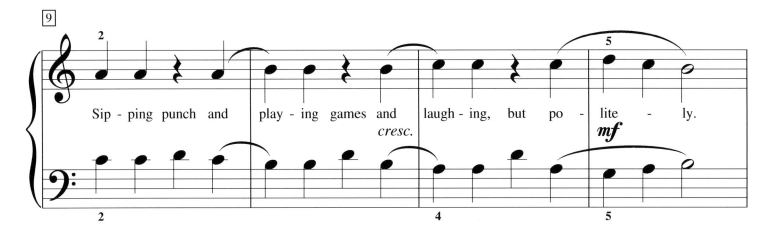

Sip-ping punch and play-ing games and laugh-ing, but po-lite-ly.

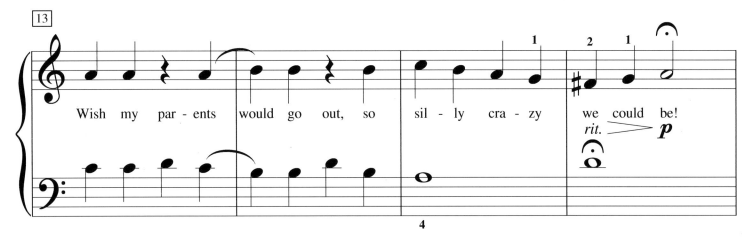

Wish my par-ents would go out, so sil-ly cra-zy we could be!

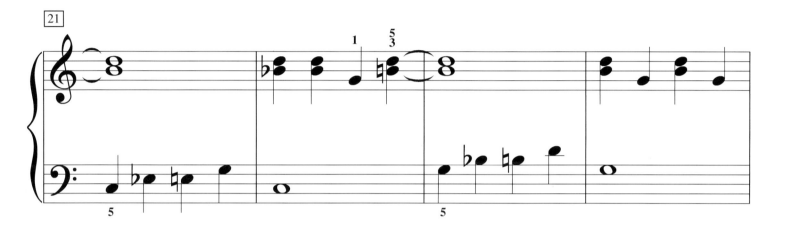

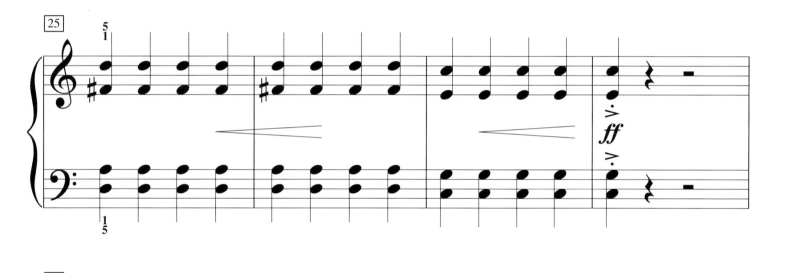

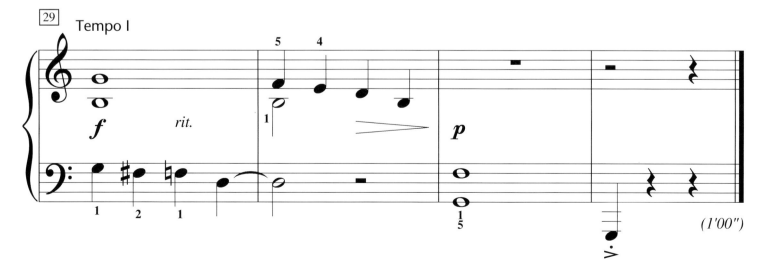

7

Pink Polka Dots

By Jennifer Linn

Lively (♩ = 144)

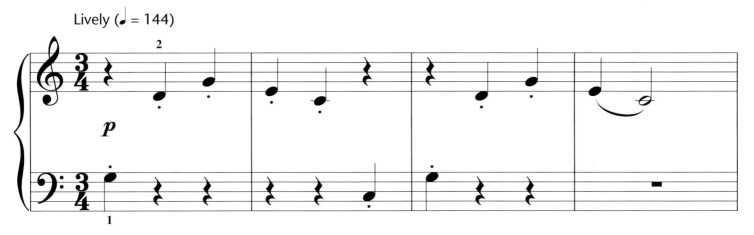

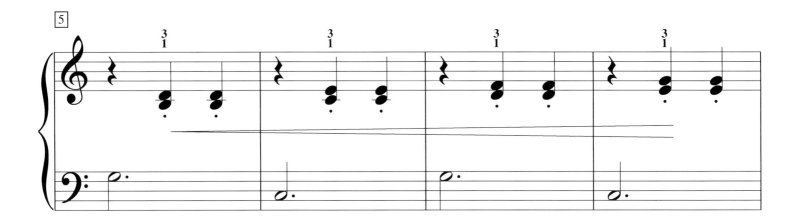

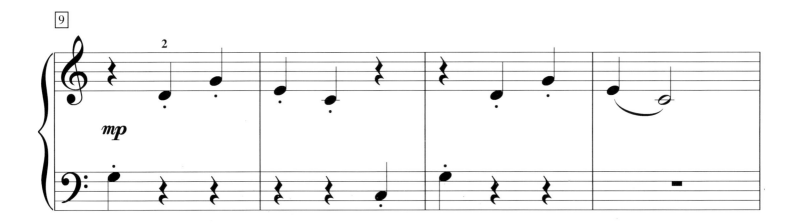

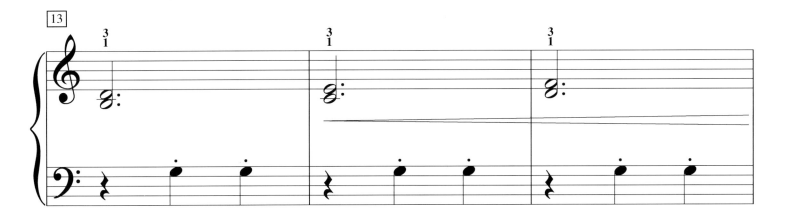

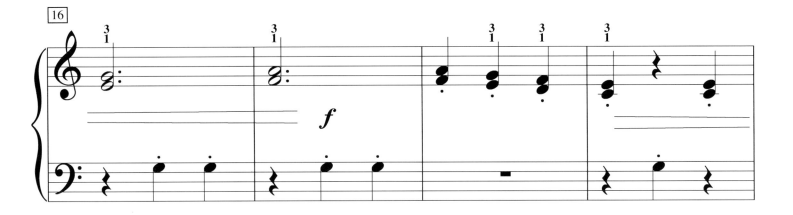

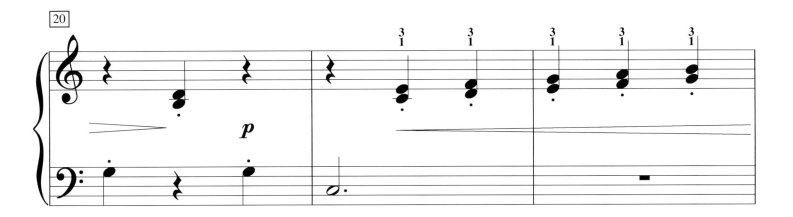

(32")

Pink Lemonade

Words and Music by
Jennifer Linn

Carefree (♩ = 100)

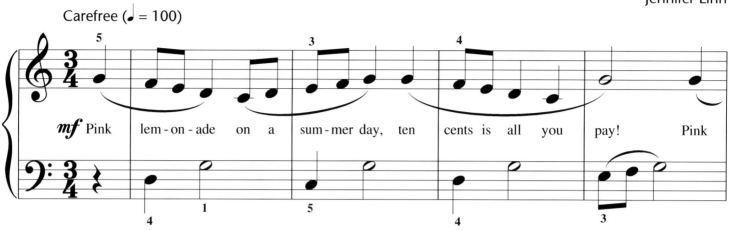

mf Pink | lem-on-ade on a | sum-mer day, ten | cents is all you | pay! Pink

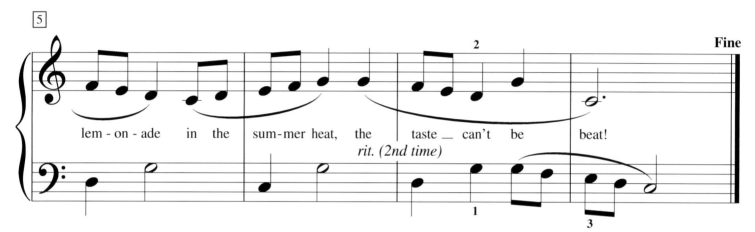

5

Fine

lem-on-ade in the | sum-mer heat, the | taste — can't be | beat!

rit. (2nd time)

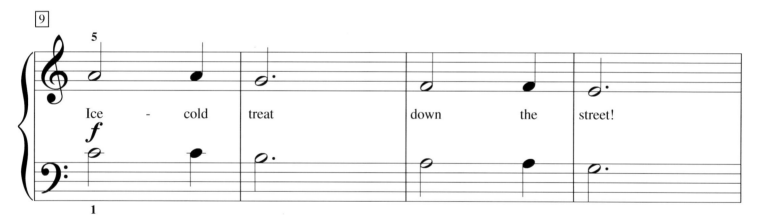

9

f

Ice - cold | treat | down the | street!

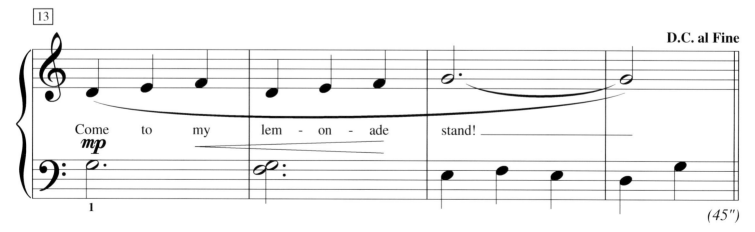

13

D.C. al Fine

mp

Come to my | lem-on-ade | stand! _____

(45″)

Rosebud

Words and Music by
Jennifer Linn

Sweetly singing (♩ = 112)

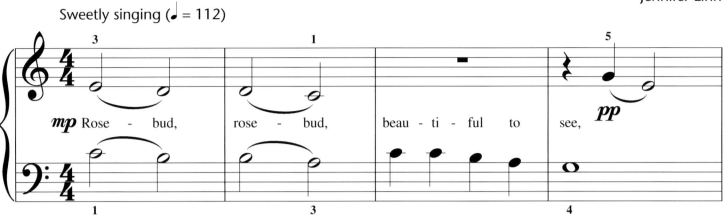

mp Rose - bud, rose - bud, beau - ti - ful to see, *pp*

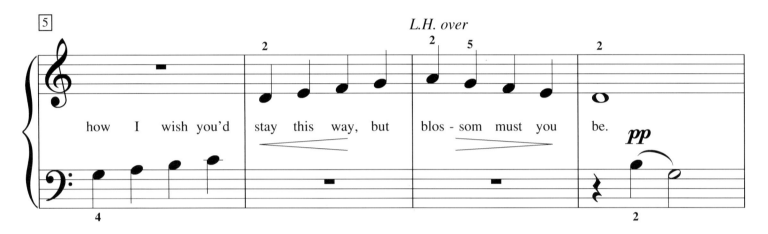

how I wish you'd stay this way, but blos - som must you be. *pp*

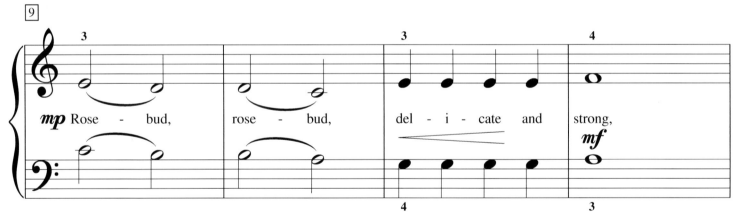

mp Rose - bud, rose - bud, del - i - cate and strong, *mf*

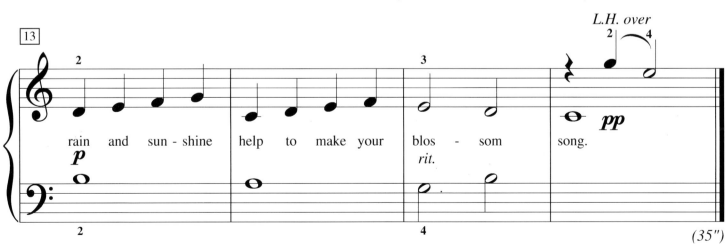

rain and sun - shine help to make your blos - som song. *pp*

p

rit.

(35")

Sunset Glow

Words and Music by
Jennifer Linn

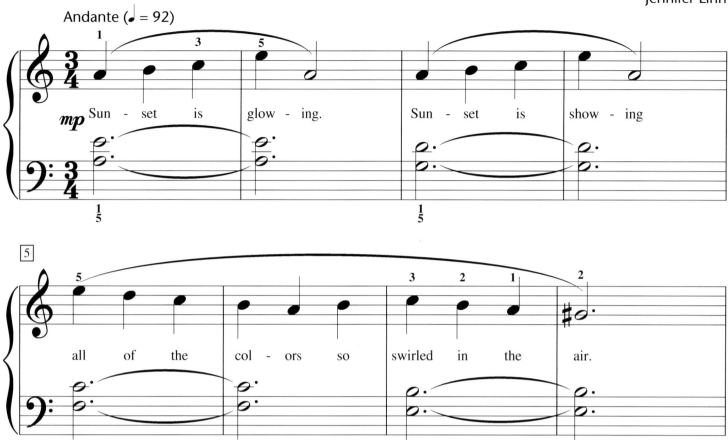

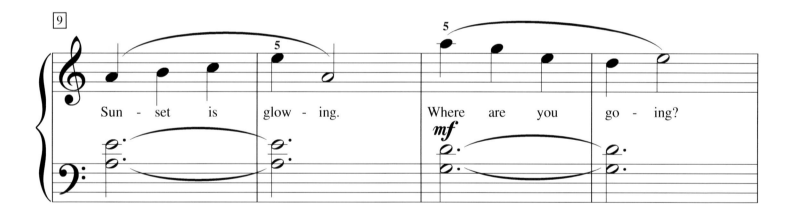

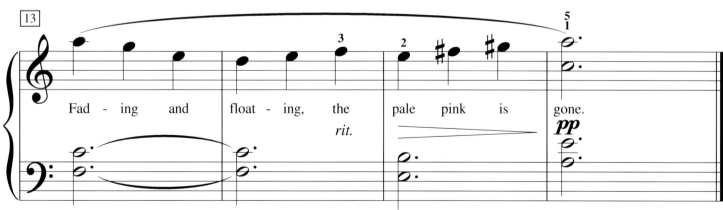

(32")

Notes from the Composer

Just Pink is a collection of fun elementary piano pieces intended to spark the imagination and create a musical connection for the young beginning student. When the musical story or "sound picture" is something a child wants to express through the piano, they are naturally motivated to overcome the challenges in the music. Practicing with a natural motivation is the goal.

With a variety of reading positions and rhythms, *Just Pink* will introduce beginning students to some new sounds, rhythms, and keyboard movements not always found in their beginning method books. These short, whimsical pieces have a fresh flavor and each one provides something new for the student to explore. The first year or two of piano study can mold a child's lifelong attitude toward music. If a student has fun playing the piano early on, practicing will be a joy for life. My hope is that this collection will make a student want to sing, to practice, to giggle, and mostly just want to have fun making music.

–Jennifer Linn

Below is a title list with a brief description of pedagogical elements found in each piece.

Bubblegum Song
- middle-C position
- damper pedal
- freedom of movement over the keyboard

Flamingo
- whole-tone scale
- damper pedal
- freedom of movement over the keyboard

Piglet
- C position with right-hand thumb shifting to B
- staccato touch
- eighth-note rhythms

Pink Fuzzy Slippers
- C position
- left-hand crossover to treble C
- eighth-note rhythms
- fermata

Pink Lemonade
- C position/middle-C position
- eighth-note rhythms
- D.C. al Fine

Pink Party Surprise
- G Position
- crossing finger 2 over finger 1
- contrasting moods
- tie over the barline
- fermata

Pink Polka Dots
- legato/staccato coordination
- 3/4 time signature
- right hand shifts in sequence
- ⎯⎯⎯⎯⎯

Rosebud
- middle-C position
- left-hand crossover
- two-note slurs (drop-lift)
- expressive playing
- ⎯⎯⎯⎯⎯

Sunset Glow
- A-minor position
- crossing finger 2 over finger 1
- expressive playing (short phrase, short phrase, long phrase)
- left-hand block fifths
- ties

COMPOSER SHOWCASE
HAL LEONARD STUDENT PIANO LIBRARY

This series showcases great original piano music from our **Hal Leonard Student Piano Library** family of composers. Carefully graded for easy selection.

BILL BOYD

JAZZ BITS (AND PIECES)
Early Intermediate Level
00290312 11 Solos......................$7.99

JAZZ DELIGHTS
Intermediate Level
00240435 11 Solos......................$8.99

JAZZ FEST
Intermediate Level
00240436 10 Solos......................$8.99

JAZZ PRELIMS
Early Elementary Level
00290032 12 Solos......................$7.99

JAZZ SKETCHES
Intermediate Level
00220001 8 Solos......................$8.99

JAZZ STARTERS
Elementary Level
00290425 10 Solos......................$8.99

JAZZ STARTERS II
Late Elementary Level
00290434 11 Solos......................$7.99

JAZZ STARTERS III
Late Elementary Level
00290465 12 Solos......................$8.99

THINK JAZZ!
Early Intermediate Level
00290417 Method Book............$12.99

TONY CARAMIA

JAZZ MOODS
Intermediate Level
00296728 8 Solos......................$6.95

SUITE DREAMS
Intermediate Level
00296775 4 Solos......................$6.99

SONDRA CLARK

DAKOTA DAYS
Intermediate Level
00296521 5 Solos......................$6.95

FLORIDA FANTASY SUITE
Intermediate Level
00296766 3 Duets......................$7.95

THREE ODD METERS
Intermediate Level
00296472 3 Duets......................$6.95

MATTHEW EDWARDS

CONCERTO FOR YOUNG PIANISTS
FOR 2 PIANOS, FOUR HANDS
Intermediate Level Book/CD
00296356 3 Movements $19.99

CONCERTO NO. 2 IN G MAJOR
FOR 2 PIANOS, 4 HANDS
Intermediate Level Book/CD
00296670 3 Movements............$17.99

PHILLIP KEVEREN

MOUSE ON A MIRROR
Late Elementary Level
00296361 5 Solos......................$8.99

MUSICAL MOODS
Elementary/Late Elementary Level
00296714 7 Solos......................$6.99

SHIFTY-EYED BLUES
Late Elementary Level
00296374 5 Solos......................$7.99

CAROL KLOSE

THE BEST OF CAROL KLOSE
Early to Late Intermediate Level
00146151 15 Solos....................$12.99

CORAL REEF SUITE
Late Elementary Level
00296354 7 Solos......................$7.50

DESERT SUITE
Intermediate Level
00296667 6 Solos......................$7.99

FANCIFUL WALTZES
Early Intermediate Level
00296473 5 Solos......................$7.95

GARDEN TREASURES
Late Intermediate Level
00296787 5 Solos......................$8.50

ROMANTIC EXPRESSIONS
Intermediate to Late Intermediate Level
00296923 5 Solos......................$8.99

WATERCOLOR MINIATURES
Early Intermediate Level
00296848 7 Solos......................$7.99

JENNIFER LINN

AMERICAN IMPRESSIONS
Intermediate Level
00296471 6 Solos......................$8.99

ANIMALS HAVE FEELINGS TOO
Early Elementary/Elementary Level
00147789 8 Solos......................$8.99

AU CHOCOLAT
Late Elementary/Early Intermediate Level
00298110 7 Solos......................$8.99

CHRISTMAS IMPRESSIONS
Intermediate Level
00296706 8 Solos......................$8.99

JUST PINK
Elementary Level
00296722 9 Solos......................$8.99

LES PETITES IMAGES
Late Elementary Level
00296664 7 Solos......................$8.99

LES PETITES IMPRESSIONS
Intermediate Level
00296355 6 Solos......................$8.99

REFLECTIONS
Late Intermediate Level
00296843 5 Solos......................$8.99

TALES OF MYSTERY
Intermediate Level
00296769 6 Solos......................$8.99

LYNDA LYBECK-ROBINSON

ALASKA SKETCHES
Early Intermediate Level
00119637 8 Solos......................$8.99

AN AWESOME ADVENTURE
Late Elementary Level
00137563 8 Solos......................$7.99

FOR THE BIRDS
Early Intermediate/Intermediate Level
00237078 9 Solos......................$8.99

WHISPERING WOODS
Late Elementary Level
00275905 9 Solos......................$8.99

MONA REJINO

CIRCUS SUITE
Late Elementary Level
00296665 5 Solos......................$8.99

COLOR WHEEL
Early Intermediate Level
00201951 6 Solos......................$9.99

IMPRESIONES DE ESPAÑA
Intermediate Level
00337520 6 Solos......................$8.99

IMPRESSIONS OF NEW YORK
Intermediate Level
00364212......................$8.99

JUST FOR KIDS
Elementary Level
00296840 8 Solos......................$7.99

MERRY CHRISTMAS MEDLEYS
Intermediate Level
00296799 5 Solos......................$8.99

MINIATURES IN STYLE
Intermediate Level
00148088 6 Solos......................$8.99

PORTRAITS IN STYLE
Early Intermediate Level
00296507 6 Solos......................$8.99

EUGÉNIE ROCHEROLLE

CELEBRATION SUITE
Intermediate Level
00152724 3 Duets......................$8.99

ENCANTOS ESPAÑOLES (SPANISH DELIGHTS)
Intermediate Level
00125451 6 Solos......................$8.99

JAMBALAYA
Intermediate Level
00296654 2 Pianos, 8 Hands.....$12.99
00296725 2 Pianos, 4 Hands.......$7.95

JEROME KERN CLASSICS
Intermediate Level
00296577 10 Solos....................$12.99

LITTLE BLUES CONCERTO
Early Intermediate Level
00142801 2 Pianos, 4 Hands......$12.99

TOUR FOR TWO
Late Elementary Level
00296832 6 Duets......................$9.99

TREASURES
Late Elementary/Early Intermediate Level
00296924 7 Solos......................$8.99

JEREMY SISKIND

BIG APPLE JAZZ
Intermediate Level
00278209 8 Solos......................$8.99

MYTHS AND MONSTERS
Late Elementary/Early Intermediate Level
00148148 9 Solos......................$8.99

CHRISTOS TSITSAROS

DANCES FROM AROUND THE WORLD
Early Intermediate Level
00296688 7 Solos......................$8.99

FIVE SUMMER PIECES
Late Intermediate/Advanced Level
00361235 5 Solos....................$12.99

LYRIC BALLADS
Intermediate/Late Intermediate Level
00102404 6 Solos......................$8.99

POETIC MOMENTS
Intermediate Level
00296403 8 Solos......................$8.99

SEA DIARY
Early Intermediate Level
00253486 9 Solos......................$8.99

SONATINA HUMORESQUE
Late Intermediate Level
00296772 3 Movements.............$6.99

SONGS WITHOUT WORDS
Intermediate Level
00296506 9 Solos......................$9.99

THREE PRELUDES
Early Advanced Level
00130747 3 Solos......................$8.99

THROUGHOUT THE YEAR
Late Elementary Level
00296723 12 Duets....................$6.95

ADDITIONAL COLLECTIONS

AT THE LAKE
by Elvina Pearce
Elementary/Late Elementary Level
00131642 10 Solos and Duets.....$7.99

CHRISTMAS FOR TWO
by Dan Fox
Early Intermediate Level
00290069 13 Duets....................$8.99

CHRISTMAS JAZZ
by Mike Springer
Intermediate Level
00296525 6 Solos......................$8.99

COUNTY RAGTIME FESTIVAL
by Fred Kern
Intermediate Level
00296882 7 Solos......................$7.99

LITTLE JAZZERS
by Jennifer Watts
Elementary/Late Elementary Level
00154573 9 Solos......................$8.99

PLAY THE BLUES!
by Luann Carman
Early Intermediate Level
00296357 10 Solos....................$9.99

ROLLER COASTERS & RIDES
by Jennifer & Mike Watts
Intermediate Level
00131144 8 Duets......................$8.99

HAL•LEONARD®
www.halleonard.com

Prices, contents, and availability subject to change without notice.

Dedicated to my daughter
Meaghan Linn